CONTENTS

PRINTED IN
DEAN &
52/54 Southwark St.
GREAT BRITAIN
SON Ltd.
LONDON SE1 1UA
TRADE MARK

Day by Day
Stories about Joseph

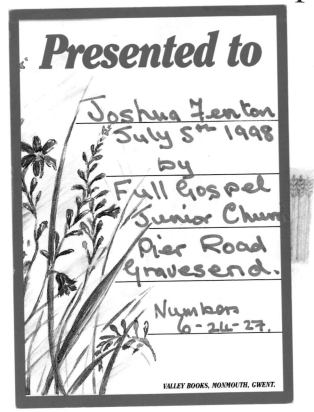

Presented to

Joshua Fenton
July 5th 1998
by
Full Gospel
Junior Church
Pier Road
Gravesend.

Numbers
6 - 24 - 27.

VALLEY BOOKS, MONMOUTH, GWENT.

Stories retold by Virginia Williams-Ellis
Illustrated by Gwen Green

© Dean & Son Ltd., 1981
ISBN 0-603-00274-9

The Coat of Many Colours

Joseph lived in the land of Canaan with his father, Jacob, and his eleven brothers. He was seventeen years old. All day he worked with his brothers, looking after the sheep.

Joseph was the second youngest brother and he was his father's favourite son. One day his father called him.

'You have always been a good son to me, Joseph, and I have made you this coat to show my love for you.'

It was a beautiful coat, woven in wool dyed many colours. Joseph was very pleased.

'Thank you, Father!' he said. 'I will always wear it!'

The other brothers were jealous because their father loved Joseph more than any of them. They began to hate him.

One night, Joseph had a dream. He told his brothers about it:

'I dreamed that we were working in the fields, binding the corn into sheaves. Suddenly, my sheaf of corn stood up, and yours all stood round it and bowed down to it.'

Joseph's brothers hated him even more for this. They began to plan how they might kill him.

A few days later the older brothers took the sheep to fields a long way from home. Jacob sent Joseph to see them. His brothers saw him in the distance coming towards them.

'This is our chance to kill him,' said one brother.

'No,' the oldest said firmly. 'We cannot kill our own brother.'

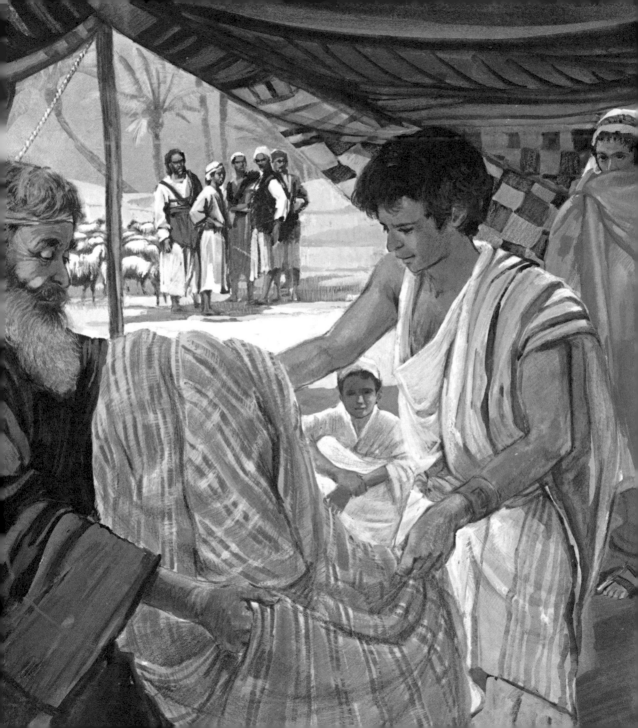

'Well, if we threw him into that deep pit over there,' one of the others said, 'and left him, he would starve to death.'

The others agreed. As Joseph came nearer he called:

'Good day, brothers! I bring greetings from our father!'

The brothers did not answer. Instead they seized him and tore off his beautiful coat. Then, grabbing him by his arms and legs, they hurled him into the great pit.

'What is the matter?' Joseph cried. 'What have I done?'

'Your dream won't come true now!' they called down to him mockingly. 'You'll never have power over us!'

Just then some spice merchants came riding past on their way to Egypt. The brothers had an idea. Pointing to Joseph, they called to the merchants:

'Here! We have a slave to sell. How much will you pay for him?'

The merchants paid twenty silver pieces. Joseph's brothers hauled him out of the pit, tied him up, and lifted him onto one of the merchant's camels.

'How can you do this to me?' Joseph shouted to them.

But they turned their backs as the merchants rode away.

The brothers stained Joseph's coat with goat's blood and took it to their father, pretending to be very worried.

'Father, we found this coat covered in blood. Is it Joseph's?'

'Yes,' Jacob cried. 'Some wild beast must have killed him.'

For many months Jacob mourned. But none of his sons had the courage to tell him what had really happened.

GENESIS, chapter 37

8

Joseph in Egypt

Potiphar was a very important man. He was captain of the guard to Pharaoh, the Egyptian King. He lived in a large, beautiful house near the palace with a great many servants to look after him.

One very hot morning Potiphar went down to the market place in the city. It was crowded and dusty, and very noisy. There were all sorts of things to buy: exotic fruits, beautiful materials, precious jewels, and even animals.

At one stall some foreign merchants were selling spices. Potiphar pushed his way to the front of the stall. As he was speaking to the merchants he noticed a boy standing silently beside them. His hands and feet were tied.

'Who is this boy?' he asked the merchants.

'He is a slave, sir, whom we bought in Canaan,' they said.

'What is your name?' Potiphar asked the boy kindly.

'I am called Joseph,' the boy answered.

Potiphar thought Joseph looked honest and intelligent.

'I will buy him as my slave,' he said.

So Joseph was untied and taken home by his new Egyptian master.

Joseph's life was not easy, but he worked hard and God was with him in all he did. Potiphar was so pleased with Joseph, he put him in charge of his entire household.

However, Potiphar's wife was jealous of Joseph and she

told her husband lies about him. When Potiphar heard the stories he became very angry.

'I will throw him into prison!' he promised his wife.

The prison was dark and dirty. Men were crowded together in small cells and quarrelled and fought. But after Joseph was put in prison, things began to change.

'Don't fight,' he told the prisoners. 'You will only make yourselves more unhappy. Try to look after one another.'

The prison keeper was so pleased with the way Joseph treated the other men that he put him in charge of them.

Among the prisoners were Pharaoh's butler and baker. One night these men both had strange dreams. Next morning, when Joseph went into their cell they looked very sad.

'We have had such strange dreams,' the butler told him, 'and we do not know what they mean.'

'God has given me the power to understand dreams,' Joseph said. 'I will explain their meanings to you.'

The men told him their dreams and Joseph explained them. The butler and baker were amazed by his wisdom.

A few days later the butler was released from the prison. As he left Joseph said to him:

'Don't forget me. I have done nothing to deserve being put in prison. Perhaps you can tell Pharaoh about me and he will free me.'

But the butler forgot all about him. So Joseph had to stay in prison for two more years.

GENESIS, chapters 39, 40

Pharaoh's Dream

Pharaoh, King of Egypt, lay sleeping in his palace. As he slept he had a strange dream. In the dream he saw seven well-fed cows coming up from a river to graze. They were followed by seven very thin cows. Then, as he watched, the thin cows devoured all the well-fed ones.

In the morning, when Pharaoh woke, he was very troubled by this dream.

'Send for all the magicians in Egypt!' he told his servants.

When all the magicians had arrived at the palace Pharaoh described his dream to them.

'Now,' he demanded, 'explain to me what this means.'

The magicians whispered together. Then one of them said:

'Your Majesty, we are sorry, we cannot explain this dream.'

'You can't explain it!' exclaimed Pharaoh angrily. 'Go away, all of you! You are of no use to me!'

News of Pharaoh's dream soon spread around the palace. When the butler heard he suddenly remembered Joseph. He went quickly to Pharaoh's chambers.

'Your Majesty,' said the butler, 'a few years ago I was in prison. Your chief baker was there too. One night we both had dreams and could not understand them. But there was a young man in the prison, who used to be a slave to Potiphar, and he explained them. And what he told us came true.'

14

'What is this man called?' Pharaoh asked him.

The butler told him and Pharaoh sent for Joseph.

'I have been told you can interpret dreams,' Pharaoh said.

'God has given me this understanding,' Joseph told him. Pharaoh then told Joseph his dream.

'The seven fat cows,' Joseph explained, 'mean that there will be seven years of very good harvests, when you must store all your spare grain. The seven thin cows mean that seven years of terrible famine will follow, when you will eat up all you have saved. This dream is a message from God, so that you can prepare for the years of famine.'

'How must we prepare ourselves?' Pharaoh asked.

'You must choose a man to organize the storing of corn throughout Egypt during the time of plenty.'

'God is obviously with you,' Pharaoh said. 'You shall be the man to do this work. You shall be in charge of my people.'

Pharaoh then dressed Joseph in fine clothes, gave him a ring from his own finger, and hung a golden chain around his neck.

Pharaoh's dream came true. For seven years the harvests were very good. Joseph travelled through Egypt and ordered the farmers to build great barns to store the spare grain. Then the terrible famine began and Joseph opened up the storehouses. People from all over the country came to buy the corn that had been saved. The Egyptians were very thankful for God's message to Pharaoh.

GENESIS, chapter 41

16

The Famine in Canaan

Meanwhile, in Canaan, Joseph's father, Jacob, had also had bad harvests. Now there was little grain left to feed the animals. Soon the family would be without food.

One day Jacob called together his eleven sons.

'I've heard that in Egypt there is plenty of food,' he told them. 'You must go to Egypt and see if you can buy some corn for us. But I will not let Benjamin, my youngest son, go with you,' he added, 'in case something happens to him. I have already lost one son, I could not bear to lose another.'

The next day Jacob's ten oldest sons set out on their donkeys for Egypt. It was a very long journey. When at last they arrived they went straight to the great hall where the grain was being sold. It was full of people pushing and arguing. Everybody wanted to be first in the queue. Many of them had travelled very long distances and they were tired and hungry.

At one end of the hall on a high platform sat the man who was selling the sacks of corn. He wore scarlet robes and a golden chain around his neck. He looked very important.

None of the brothers realised it was Joseph.

When at last their turn came they went up to the platform and knelt down. As soon as Joseph saw his brothers he recognized them, but he pretended not to know them.

'Where have you come from?' he asked them roughly.

'From Canaan,' they replied.

'I think you are spies!' Joseph accused them. 'You have come to spy out the land.'

'We are not spies!' they said. 'We are ten honest brothers. Our youngest brother is at home. We have come to buy food.'

'I shall not believe you are speaking the truth,' Joseph said, 'until you bring your brother to me. One of you must stay as prisoner until you return with the boy.'

His brothers pleaded with him but Joseph took no notice. He chose his brother, Simeon, as prisoner. Then he filled up their sacks with corn and they paid him for it.

'Now, go back and fetch your brother,' he ordered.

While his brothers were preparing to leave Joseph secretly said to his servant:

'Take the silver that these men gave for their grain and put it in the top of their sacks. I do not want them to be short of money on their journey.'

The nine brothers set out sadly back to Canaan. On their way they stopped at an inn and opened their sacks to feed their donkeys. When they saw the money on top of the corn they were amazed and afraid.

'How did it get there?' they asked one another. 'This must be the work of God. It is all happening because of what we did to our brother Joseph.'

They travelled home with heavy hearts.

GENESIS, chapter 42

The Feast

Jacob was very worried when his sons told him that Benjamin too must now go to Egypt.

'First Joseph was killed, then Simeon captured, and now you want to take Benjamin away from me,' he said sadly. 'It is too much to ask of an old man.'

But very soon nearly all the grain his sons had bought in Egypt was finished.

'We must go back for more,' his sons urged him. 'And if we don't take Benjamin the man won't let us buy any more. Simeon will be kept as his prisoner.'

'All right,' Jacob agreed at last, 'but when you go, take the man a present—a little honey, spices and myrrh, figs and almonds. And take twice the amount of money to pay him back for the silver you found in your sacks. Perhaps, then, he will be good to you and send all my sons back to me again.'

So the brothers travelled to Egypt once more, taking Benjamin with them. When Joseph saw that they had returned he said to the head of his household:

'Take these men to my home and prepare a feast. They are to eat with me today.'

The brothers were very surprised that this important man was treating them as his special guests. When they arrived at Joseph's house his servants gave them water, so that they could wash their feet, and fed their donkeys for them. Then

their brother, Simeon, was brought in to join them. They were all very pleased to see him again.

When Joseph arrived home his brothers knelt and gave him their presents. Joseph asked them how their father was.

'He is very well, sir,' they answered.

'And this is the young boy, Benjamin, you told me about,' said Joseph, looking lovingly at his younger brother. 'God bless you,' he said to him.

Joseph was suddenly overcome with love for his family. He left the room quickly to find a place to weep by himself. He did not want them to guess yet that he was their brother.

'How much I have missed them all,' he thought.

Then he washed and went back to the room.

'Now, we will eat!' he said cheerfully.

Joseph seated his brothers around the table in the order of their ages. They were amazed.

'How does he know how old we all are?' they wondered.

Joseph himself sat on a separate table. But he talked with them during the meal, laughed with them, and called the servants to bring more food and wine as soon as their plates and goblets were empty. There was plenty to eat and drink for everyone but Joseph ordered Benjamin to be given five times more than the others because he loved him so much. He was so happy that they were all together again. Yet still none of them realized he was their brother.

GENESIS, chapter 43

A New Home in Egypt

Joseph's brothers slept soundly after the feast. When they were in bed Joseph called his steward.

'Fill these men's sacks with as much food as they can carry. Then put the money each has paid in the top of each sack. And put my silver cup in Benjamin's sack.'

As dawn broke next day Joseph's eleven brothers set off on their donkeys towards home. They had not gone far when they heard a horse behind them. They turned to see Joseph's steward following.

'Stop!' he shouted. 'One of you has stolen my master's cup!'

The brothers were astounded.

'Whoever has stolen the silver cup must return to be my master's servant,' the man said.

The brothers climbed down and quickly opened their sacks. The steward searched through them all and came at last to Benjamin's. When the brothers saw the cup in Benjamin's sack they were very upset. Slowly they remounted their donkeys and returned to Joseph's house.

'My lord,' they said, kneeling at Joseph's feet. 'We do not know how the cup came to be in the sack. We would never have stolen from you. Please don't keep Benjamin as your servant. Our father will die if he does not go home to him. We would all rather stay than leave Benjamin behind.'

When Joseph saw how much his brothers cared for

Benjamin he was overcome with love for them all. He ordered his attendants to leave. Then he broke down and cried.

'I am your brother Joseph!' he told them.

His brothers were so surprised, they could say nothing.

'Do not be upset any longer for what you did to me. It was God's plan just as He showed me long ago in my dream. He sent me here to do this work so I could save you from the famine.'

Joseph then embraced them and told them all that had happened to him.

'Now, go home quickly and bring our father and your families back here. There are still five years of famine to come and I shall make sure you have all you need.'

When Jacob heard that Joseph was still alive he was filled with happiness. He and his family packed their belongings onto wagons and journeyed towards their new home.

Joseph was so impatient to see his father that he rode out in his chariot to meet him. When he saw Jacob he leapt down and ran and threw his arms around him.

'Praise God!' said Jacob joyfully. 'Now I have all my sons with me again!'

Pharaoh granted Joseph's family the best land in the country where they could settle. And so for many years Jacob and all his descendants lived in Egypt, until the time when Moses led the Israelites to the promised land.

GENESIS, chapters 44, 45, 46, 47

28